Blind Faith is exactly what is says: Going for your dreams and having absolute belief that it will work out in your favor.

GOAL-SETTING WORKBOOK

To You, From Me...

Personal Promise:

I solemnly promise to make the best effort in seeking out every opportunity for my dreams. I CAN DO THIS! If I don't make this happen, it won't happen. The first step is here; the rest is up to me.

Dreamer _____

Dreamer Witness _____

Date _____

Copyright © 2020 Dr. Denise Y. Mose

All rights reserved. No part of this book may be reproduced or transmitted in any form or by any means, electronically or mechanically, including photocopying, recording, or by an information storage and retrieval system without permission in writing from the author of this book.

ISBN:

Published by:

Edited by:

Spirit of Excellence Writing & Editing Services, LLC

www.TakeUpThySword.com

HOW TO USE THIS WORKBOOK

In this workbook, you will find the following worksheets to help your dreams go from ACTUAL TO FACTUAL! I designed this to help you focus. Are you ready to do this? I am!

1. VISION BOARD: Neon green, orange, purple, yellow, powder blue or even bright red - Colors have power. Head to the nearest supply store and pick out the color that speaks to you. Here's the thing: you must see it in your mind before you can go out and conquer that dream physically. By that, I mean complete HONESTY! This sheet offers clarity, light, personal intuition, and direction as you move forward. Your core values are the center of your essence.

2. SELF-ASSESSMENT: No one knows you better than...YOU! However, I don't want you to lie to yourself. Look in the mirror and be candid. What do you do well? What needs work? This structure allows you to work as your inspiration flows and still accomplish big, amazing dreams each quarter. Also, write where you see yourself in the future. Don't have a filter. No dream is too big. GO FOR IT. On the following pages, together, we will get you there.

3. CREATE CONTACTS: Look, I know you are "Big and Bad" and totally awesome. Here's the thing though: dreams need a little help. Do you know who is on your team? Like, someone who you KNOW believes in you no matter the situation? Did you know that most people don't have someone like that? Take out your phone and really see each name. What's the first emotion that comes to mind about that contact? On this journey of dreams, you don't have time to play around. Who is organized and punctual? Who are the Globetrotters? Who is a stable influence? Write each name down and identify one word that best describes that contact. Start there.

4. YOUR AFFIRMATIONS: These beautiful words are here to remind you that you made the right decision. YOU CAN AND WILL DO THIS! Let these words assist you along the way. Say each affirmation out loud. Memorize it. Feel it. Own it.

5. MOVE WITH MUSIC: Music is therapy! I'm not endorsing any artist here, but please do yourself a favor and choose some good music as we take this journey. It is soul-nourishing! Examine your vison board and allow the tunes to inspire you.

6. ACCOUNTABILITY: At this point, we've done the grit work. Now, let's put it into action. Get a big wall calendar. Realistically, put dates and names beside your goal: New website? Book release? Cookie recipes? Nutrition podcast? Secure passport? Make that key phone call? Write your business plan? IT...IS...GO...TIME!

7. ACTION PLAN: This is your GOAL-SETTING PAGE! We did it; we are here. Detail is paramount. Notate each dream and fine-tune that goal. Put the date by each goal that you completed. Also, breathe. Rome was not built in a day, but it did get built. Display your Action Plan on your wall and work through each area. Last thing…Celebrate!

The best goals are the following…

1. BIG
2. CLEAR-CUT
3. MEASURABLE
4. ATTAINABLE
5. FULFILLING
6. TRACKABLE

"Every tub has to sit on its own bottom" –
Mr. Daniel Mose, Sr., Beloved Grandfather

You owe it to yourself to attempt the impossible…

VISION BOARD
DO NOT HOLD BACK!!! MAKE IT VISUAL!!!

Your Assignment:

1. Buy a large piece of cardboard.
2. Get magazines and newspapers.
3. Cut out the life you see for yourself.
4. Glue onto your Vision Board.
5. Take a picture of yourself - that goes in the middle.
6. Respond, reflect and react on this...daily.

SELF-ASSESSMENT

This document helps you think about YOURSELF. You can identify your Short-Term and Long-Term Goals. Be honest.

My Strengths	**My Weaknesses**
_____	_____
_____	_____
_____	_____

My Worth Ethic

_____

_____

_____

My Values and Beliefs

_____

_____

_____

Short-Term Goal
(less than 6 months)

_____

_____

_____

Long-Term Goal
(year or more)

_____

_____

_____

Must Haves

_____

_____

_____

Areas of Negotiation

_____

_____

_____

Conflict Resolution

_____

_____

_____

Diversity of Community

_____

_____

_____

CREATE CONTACTS

Dreams are a beautiful thing, but you will need help getting there. I'm going to get you started; you fill in the rest. You know your core of friends, contacts, and associates better than anyone. Are they ready to take this journey with you? Let's find out.

Name:	John	**Name:**	Danielle
Job:	Musician	**Job:**	Accountant
Core:	Problem-Solver	**Core:**	No Sugar-Coating
Name:	K. Morris	**Name:**	Monique
Job:	Lawyer	**Job:**	Entertainment Guru
Core:	Deals in Facts	**Core:**	Highly Creative

Name: _____   **Name:** _____

Job: _____   **Job:** _____

Core: _____   **Core:** _____

Name: _____   **Name:** _____

Job: _____   **Job:** _____

Core: _____   **Core:** _____

Name: _____   **Name:** _____

Job: _____   **Job:** _____

Core: _____   **Core:** _____

Name: _____   **Name:** _____

Job: _____   **Job:** _____

Core: _____   **Core:** _____

YOUR AFFIRMATIONS

ADVENTURE	LEARNING
AMBITION	LOVE
AUTHORITY	MORALS
AUTONOMY	NO LIMIT
BALANCE	OPTIMISTIC
BEAUTY	PASSION
BIG	PEACE
BOLDNESS	PERSISTENCE
BRAVERY	PRAY
BRILLIANCE	PURPOSE
CALM	QUANTITY
CHALLENGE	RESPECT
COMPASSION	RESPONSIBILITY
COMPETENCY	SECURITY
CREATIVITY	SERVICE
DESIRE	STABLE
FAITH	SUCCESS
FEARLESS	TIMELINE
FUN	TRANSPARENT
HAPPINESS	TRUST
HONESTY	WEALTH
IMAGINATION	WISDOM
INDIVIDUALITY	WORK
INNOVATION	X-FACTOR
JOY	YOUTH
KINDNESS	ZEAL

SHORT-TERM GOALS

Short-Term Goals are completed in less than six months. Let's get the ball rolling...

Quarter 1	Quarter 2
Goal 1: Date: Goal 2: Date: Goal 3:	Goal 1: Date: Goal 2: Date: Goal 3:
Quarter 3	**Quarter 4**
Goal 1: Date: Goal 2: Date: Goal 3: Date:	Goal 1: Date: Goal 2: Date: Goal 3: Date:

Because I am colossally right-brained, I need to physically see my thoughts to keep my goals centered. Therefore, I offer you this guideline to aide you when inspiration strikes!

ACTION PLAN: BECAUSE YOU HAVE NO TIME TO WASTE...

Making the Invisible...Visible

Goal (In 1-5 Words)

Steps You'll Take to Get There:

1.

2.

3.

4.

Measure Your Progress:

Current Date:

Completion Date:

Resources Needed:

Financial:

Sweat Equity:

Result:

Benefits of Reaching My Goal:

1.

2.

3.

4.

Track Your Progress!

Timeline:

First Step (s):

Mid-Way Progress Mark:

Additional Milestones:

*

*

*

YOU DID IT!

Bring on the Bubbly!

Dream Witness: _____

GOAL CHECKLIST

Goal: _____

Date: _____

Motivation:
_____
_____
_____

Currently my job is: _____

Steps to Take:

1.

2.

3.

4.

Yes/No: I have shared my disappointments with those whom I know care about me.
Yes/No: Being transparent is difficult.
Yes/No: I'm not sure I can really accomplish all that I feel I deserve.
Yes/No: I need to remove people and things in order get focused.
Yes/No: I will share my progress.

Dream Witness: _____

GOAL CHECKLIST

Goal: _____

Date: _____

Motivation:
_____
_____
_____

Currently my job is: _____

Steps to Take:

1.

2.

3.

4.

Yes/No: I must stop measuring my success by others.

Yes/No: My Dream can happen, and it will.

Yes/No: Failure scares me.

Yes/No: I give up too easily.

Yes/No: I will take walks by myself to allow thoughts to circulate.

Dream Witness: _____

GOAL CHECKLIST

Goal: _____

Date: _____

Motivation:
_____
_____
_____

Currently my job is: _____

Steps to Take:

1.

2.

3.

4.

Yes/No: I need to secure a mentor who believes in me wholeheartedly.
Yes/No: I must know that the first investment is ME.
Yes/No: I do not care about other people's opinions.
Yes/No: I still need to remove people and things in order get focused.
Yes/No: I will assist someone with their future Dream.

Dream Witness: _____

GOAL CHECKLIST

Goal: _____

Date: _____

Motivation:
_____
_____
_____

Currently my job is: _____

Steps to Take:

1.

2.

3.

4.

Yes/No: I will write down small accomplishments.
Yes/No: My inner circle must change.
Yes/No: My passport is up to date.
Yes/No: My fears will stop me if I let them.
Yes/No: I will continue to share my progress.

Dream Witness: _____

ALMOST THERE....

My desire for you is to reach every single Dream that you can DREAM! Life is so very short. You've wasted enough time, right? Let's stop that today. Trust me, I've been there. You are talking to someone who let it all go and believed in herself. You know why? I had no other choice than to bet on that woman in the mirror.

I believed in her and that was the push I needed. Now, I'm giving it to you.

Thank you for allowing me to help you with your Dream. For more information about me, please visit my social sites under Dr. Denise Y. Mose. Please check there for all my Upcoming Tours, TV appearances, Presentations, Meet & Greets, Newsletters, and the latest on where to find me. The accompaniment to this workbook, "Blind Faith," is a wonderful addition to your Dream Journey and chronicles how I dropped everything and traveled to China for some much needed Self-Discovery.

This has been my joy to create for you. Your Dream is waiting.

Denise "Dr. D" Mose, Ph.D

www.ingramcontent.com/pod-product-compliance
Lightning Source LLC
Chambersburg PA
CBHW060307010526
44108CB00041B/2590